# Aristocr
# A Study of the Rights, the Origin, and the Social Functions of the Wealthier Classes
# (Part-II)

W. H. Mallock

Alpha Editions

This Edition Published in 2021

ISBN: 9789355759320

Design and Setting By
**Alpha Editions**
www.alphaedis.com
Email – info@alphaedis.com

As per information held with us this book is in Public Domain.
This book is a reproduction of an important historical work.
Alpha Editions uses the best technology to reproduce historical
work in the PR-same manner it was first published to preserve its
original nature. Any marks or number seen are left intentionally to
preserve its true form.

# TABLE OF CONTENTS

# PREFACE

The word *aristocracy* as used in the title of this volume has no exclusive, and indeed no special reference to a class distinguished by hereditary political privileges, by titles, or by heraldic pedigree. It here means the exceptionally gifted and efficient minority, no matter what the position in which its members may have been born, or what the sphere of social progress in which their exceptional efficiency shows itself. I have chosen the word *aristocracy* in preference to the word *oligarchy* because it means not only the rule of the few, but of the best or the most efficient of the few.

Of the various questions involved in the general argument of the work, many would, if they were to be examined exhaustively, demand entire treatises to themselves rather than chapters. This is specially true of such questions as the nature of men's congenital inequalities, the effects of different classes of motive in producing different classes of action, and the effects of equal education on unequal talents and temperaments. But the practical bearings of an argument are more readily grasped when its various parts are set forth with comparative brevity, than they are when the attention claimed for each is minute enough to do it justice as a separate subject of inquiry; and it has appeared to me that in the present condition of opinion, prevalent social fallacies may be more easily combated by putting the case against them in a form which will render it intelligible to everybody, and by leaving many points to be elaborated, if necessary, elsewhere.

I may also add that the conclusions here arrived at, with whatever completeness they might have been explained, elaborated, and defended, would not, in my opinion, do more than partially answer the questions to which they refer. This volume aims only at establishing what are the social rights and social functions, in progressive communities, of the few. The entire question of their duties and proper liabilities, whether imposed on them by themselves or by the State, has been left untouched. This side of the question I hope to deal with hereafter. It is enough to observe here that it is impossible to define the duties of the few, of the rich, of the powerful, of the highly gifted, and to secure that these duties shall be performed by them, unless we first understand the extent of the functions which they inevitably perform, and admit frankly the indefeasible character of their rights.

# BOOK II

# CHAPTER I
## THE NATURE AND DEGREES OF THE
## SUPERIORITIES OF GREAT MEN

That great men are true causes of progress is admitted by Mr. Spencer himself to be the natural opinion of mankind. What has been done, then, in the preceding book is not much more than this:—a sound popular judgment, which is of the highest sociological importance, has been rescued from the discredit cast on it by the sophisms of modern theorists. These very theorists themselves, when they reason as practical men, have been shown to the reader blowing all their disproofs of it to the winds, and holding and appealing to it as tenaciously and as passionately as anybody; and it is consequently given back to us, with its old authority unimpaired. Sound popular judgments, however, are not science. They lack what is the essence of science—that is to say, analytical precision. We must now, therefore, take this judgment with regard to the great man, and endeavour to invest it with a meaning exact and full enough to enable us to apply it to the detailed phenomena of society.

And here Mr. Herbert Spencer shall once more help us; for this remarkable writer, though he fails to recognise what he is doing, not only appeals on many critical occasions to the great-man theory as an explanation of the most important social phenomena, but he is repeatedly calling attention throughout his sociological writings to those facts of human nature of which the great-man theory is the expression. It will be sufficient to quote a few passages only.

Let us turn, then, to the opening pages of Mr. Spencer's *Study of Sociology* and consider what is contained in them. We shall find that they are entirely devoted to describing the abject mental condition of by far the largest portion of all classes of English society, from the labourer, the farmer, and the Nonconformist minister with his Bible, up to "men called educated" and the most illustrious of our historians and philosophers. All of them, says Mr. Spencer, "*are slaves to unwarranted opinions*"; "*proximate causes*" are all that the majority of them are able to understand. Nor does he represent this as some accidental result, due to prejudices or deficiencies in education peculiar to our own country. He represents it as an inevitable result of the character of the human race. In his "*Postscript*" to the same volume he takes care to make his meaning plain. "*Most people*," he says, "*conclude quickly from small evidence*," and are incapable "*of comprehending in their totality assembled propositions.*" Indeed, those whose mental constitution is such that they can take a rational view of "*human affairs*" are, he proceeds to say, merely "*a scattered few.*" He elsewhere divides society into "*the capable and the incapable,*" the "*worthy and the unworthy*"; and in the "*Postscript*" just alluded to he mentions as an admitted fact that in every social aggregate "*the inferior form the majority.*" But a yet more caustic passage remains to be mentioned. In this same work, *The Study of Sociology*, he is ridiculing—and very justly—the socialistic idea that the State can be endowed with any talent or wisdom beyond what happens to be possessed by the individual functionaries who compose the State. These functionaries, he says, are merely "*a cluster of men,*" which, like any other cluster taken at hap-hazard, will comprise "*a few clever individuals, many ordinary, some decidedly stupid*"; and he devotes pages to showing by means of multiplied examples, how incapable the ordinary statesman, to say nothing of the decidedly stupid, has been of promoting progress in even the simplest ways.

Mankind at large, then, according to Mr. Spencer, may, roughly speaking, be divided into three classes—the "*clever*" who are few, the "*ordinary*" who are the bulk of the population, and the "*decidedly stupid*" who form a considerable residuum; and it will appear from what he says of that representative "*cluster,*" the State, that whilst all real progress is the work of the clever few, the "*ordinary men*" do nothing to promote it, and "*the decidedly stupid men*" impede it.

Now it must be perfectly obvious to the reader that in this description of mankind we have the fundamental facts before us which the great-man theory formulates. For let us begin by supposing that the entire human race contained no individuals superior to the "*decidedly stupid,*" who, whenever they are placed in official positions, do nothing, Mr. Spencer declares, but commit the most pernicious blunders, either by their irrational conservatism, or their still more irrational innovations. It is obvious that in this case the world would never have progressed at all. Let us next suppose that in addition to the "*decidedly stupid*" men, the human race comprises also a large proportion of "*ordinary*" men, but not a single man who deserves to be called more than "*ordinary.*" Could social progress, as we know it, have taken place even then? Could thought, for example, ever have made any advances, had everybody been as incapable as Mr. Spencer's "*ordinary*" man is of taking a rational view of human affairs—had everybody been enslaved, like him, "*to unwarranted opinions,*" and been, like him, entirely lacking in the faculty which enables a man to comprehend *"assembled propositions in their totality"*? Or to put the whole matter in terms of a single instance, could Mr. Spencer's own system of philosophy have been written if he himself had not been immensely superior not only to *"ordinary"* men, but even to those rival thinkers whom, in every one of his volumes, he treats with such supreme disdain?

The answer of course is No. Under such conditions progress would have been quite impossible. Our simple argument will accordingly run thus. It is evident that those triumphs of thought, enterprise, and invention, to which social progress is due, could never have been made had the whole of each generation been as stupid and void of character as its lowest and weakest members. Therefore progress must be due to men who are superior to the *"decidedly stupid."* Here we have the great-man theory in embryo. But it is equally evident that we can go a step farther, and say that progress could never have taken place had there been no individuals who in will, originality, and intellect were superior to *"ordinary men."* Social progress, therefore, must be due to this third class—the class which alone is capable of taking *"a rational"* view of things; but this class, as Mr. Spencer tells us, consists of a *"scattered few,"* and here we have, in Mr. Spencer's own language, neither more nor less than the great-man theory developed. We have it developed in the form of a distinct general proposition that progress is due not to mankind at large, but to a minority of exceptional individuals, and in this form, which Mr. Spencer has assisted us in giving it, it is brought into actual accordance with the facts of social life, and, unlike the wild exaggerations of Carlyle, it will be found to accord the more closely with them the more fully it is analysed.

The error of writers like Carlyle was that they took a part for the whole. They recognised no great men at all except great men of the greatest kind—heroic figures which appeared once or twice in a century; and as for the rest of mankind, they treated them, in accordance with Mr. Spencer's formula, as a mass of units, approximately equal in capacity. The truth of the case is, on the contrary, this:—that whatever is done by great men of the heroic type, something similar, if not so striking, is done by a number of lesser great men also; that whilst the action of the heroic great men is intermittent, the action of the lesser great men is constant; and that the latter, as a body, although not individually, do incalculably more to promote progress than the former.

Let us accordingly make it perfectly clear that when we describe great men as being a minority, or a *"scattered few,"* we do not mean that out of every thousand men there are nine hundred and ninety-nine *"ordinary"* men and one genius; or that there are (let us say) seven hundred who can be described for all purposes as *"ordinary,"* and two hundred and ninety-nine who can be for all purposes described as *"stupid"*; and that there is one *"clever"* or *"great"* man who towers over them like an oak tree over bramble bushes. Nor, again, do we mean that *"greatness"* is some single definite quality, which marks its possessor out like a white man amongst negroes. Believers in extreme democracy, who very rightly discern in the great-man theory the destruction of their favourite enthusiasms, will instinctively seek to attribute some meaning such as this to its exponents. But the great-man theory, when properly analysed and explained, will be found to comprise no such absurdities as the foregoing. When we speak of "greatness" we mean a great variety of efficiencies, which, though grouped together because they are all exceptional in degree, are nevertheless indefinitely various in kind; and, moreover, the degrees to which they are exceptional are indefinitely various also, the degree being in many cases so low that it is difficult to say whether it should be classed as exceptional at all. In short, there are as many degrees of greatness as there are of temperature; and it is as difficult to draw a line between ordinary men and men whose greatness is of a very low degree, as it is to draw a line between coldness, coolness, and low degrees of heat. But though it may be questionable whether we should call a day cool when the thermometer is at fifty-nine, and whether we should call it hot when the thermometer is at sixty-one, everybody admits that it is hot when the thermometer is at eighty-five, and cold when the thermometer registers twenty degrees of frost. In the same way, though there will be a certain number of people who may be classed as great by one judge and classed as ordinary by another, there is a certain number whose capacities, however unequal amongst themselves, set their possessors apart as indubitably greater than the majority; and we are speaking with sufficient, though we cannot speak with absolute precision, when we say that progress depends on the action of this minority.

How great the inequality is between the natural powers of men is perhaps most clearly evidenced by the case of art, and more especially the art of poetry. In certain domains of effort it may be urged that unequal results are caused by unequal circumstances, quite as much as by unequal capacities. But about poetry, at all events, this cannot be said. Some of the greatest poets the world has ever known—it is enough to instance the cases of Burns and Shakespeare—have been men of no wealth and of very imperfect education. Obviously, therefore, in poetry one man has as good a chance as another. It is no doubt often argued—and this argument has already been examined—that great poets, of whom Shakespeare is a favourite example, owe part of their greatness not to themselves, but to their age. But this does nothing to explain the differences between poets who belong to the same age, and who, all of them, in this respect, start with the same advantage. Let us confine our comparisons then to men who were each other's contemporaries, and ask what made Burns a better poet than Pye, Shakespeare a greater poet than the feeblest of his forgotten rivals, Pope than Ambrose Philips, Byron than *"the hoarse Fitzgerald"*? There is only one answer possible. These men in respect of poetry had been made giants by nature; those were condemned by nature to live and to die dwarfs.

And the same inequality that exhibits itself in the domain of poetry will be found in every other domain of human effort. What can be more unequal than the gifts of different singers? In every school and university we see multitudes of young men and boys whose opportunities of learning are not only similar but identical, but of whom, in respect to assimilating what they are taught, not one in ten rises appreciably above a certain level, and not one in a hundred rises above it signally. We have Virgil at one end of the scale, and Bavius and Mævius at the other; at one end Patti, and the other the vocalist of the street; at one end a Scaliger and a Newton, and at the other the idler and the dunce, who can hardly conjugate τυπτω or stumble across the Asses' Bridge. And in practical life the same phenomenon repeats itself. Let us take any department of social activity or production, on the results of which the welfare of society at any given time depends. Let us take, for instance, the work of government, or invention, or commercial enterprise. In each of these we shall find a large number of men, each doing what is in him to subserve some particular end; and we shall find a few producing results which are great both for themselves and others, and the many producing results which are uniform in their individual pettiness.

It is perfectly true that in these great departments of practical life there may not be so obvious or so widely extended an equality of opportunity as that which prevails amongst poets, or amongst scholars in the same seminary, but in each department there will be a large number, at all events, whose opportunities are as equal as human ingenuity could make them. This is so in the French army, in the English House of Commons, and in the world of business and industry; and yet of men thus equally placed we see some doing great things, and doubling their opportunities by using them; others doing little or nothing, and throwing their opportunities away. We have accordingly in every domain of activity a sufficient number of persons with the same external advantages, to show by the extraordinary difference between the results accomplished by them how great the natural inequality between men's capacities is, and how far the efficiency of a few exceeds that of the majority. It is therefore nothing to the purpose to attribute, as many reformers do, men's inequality in efficiency to the fact that equality of opportunity is not at present as general as it theoretically might be. To extend this equality further might produce good results or bad; but in neither case would it tend to make men's capacities equal. The utmost it would do in this particular respect would be merely to widen the area of their realised inequality—to increase the number of the mountains, not to produce a plain.

It will doubtless be objected by those who would minimise natural inequalities that a man may be contemptible in one capacity—that of a poet, for instance—and yet be greater as a man than men who in one capacity are superior to him. It may, for example, be said that Frederick of Prussia, in spite of his bad poetry, was a greater man than Voltaire. This is perfectly true; but it is necessary to explain clearly that it in no way contradicts what is being here asserted. It is, on the contrary, part of it. It cannot be too emphatically said that greatness, in the only sense in which we are here considering it—that is to say, as an agent of social progress—is a quality which we attribute to a man not with reference to his whole nature, but with reference solely to the objective results produced by him, so that in one domain of activity a man may be great, in another ordinary, in another decidedly stupid. What, then, we here mean by a great man is merely a man who is superior to the majority in his power of producing some given class of result, whereas the average man and the stupid are not superior to the majority in their powers of producing any.

The reader must thus entirely disabuse himself of the idea that greatness, as an agent of social progress, has any necessary resemblance to greatness as conceived of by the moralist. A man may be a great saint or a noble "moral character" who passes his life in obscurity, stretched on a bed of sickness, and incapable even of rendering the humblest help to others. He is great in virtue not of what he does, but of what he is. But greatness, as an agent of social progress, has nothing whatever to do with what a man is, except in so far as what he is enables him to do what he does. If two doctors were confronted by some terrible epidemic, and the one met it by tending the poor for nothing, and died in his unavailing efforts to save his patients, whilst the other fled from the infected district, and solacing himself at a distance with a mistress and an excellent cook, invented a medicine by which the disease could be warded off, and proceeded to make a large fortune by selling it, though the former as a man might be incalculably better than the latter, the latter as an agent of progress would be incalculably greater than the former. Again, if two doctors tried to invent such a medicine, and whilst the first succeeded the second failed, the second, though he might have exerted himself far more than the first, and have failed only owing to some minute flaw in his faculties, would be not only less great as an agent of progress than the first, but he would not be practically an agent of progress at all, any more than a man is an agent in saving another from drowning if he merely stretches a hand which the drowning man cannot reach, and actually himself tumbles into the water in doing so.

This truth, which sounds brutal when plainly stated, but is really little more than a sociological truism, is constantly overlooked, and even indignantly denied, by thinkers whose emotions are more powerful than their minds. The way in which such persons reason is very easily understood. They see that a number of men by whom great social results are produced—men who make successful inventions and who found great businesses—are narrow-minded, uncultivated, and contemptible in general conversation, and that a number of other men who produce no such results are scholars, critics, thinkers, keen judges of men and things; and contrasting the brilliancy of those who have produced no great social results with the narrow ideas and dulness of those who have produced many, they proceed to argue that great social results cannot possibly require great men to produce them; or, in other words, that they might be produced by almost anybody.

But the whole of this class of objections will altogether disappear when we more closely examine what the qualities are on which the production of given social results depends. Let us take a few of these results as examples. Let us take the formulation and the popularising of some particular political demand, by which the whole course of a country's history is affected, and the increasing and cheapening the supply of some articles of popular consumption—sugar, let us say, or workmen's boots and clothing. The persons who urge the objections we are now discussing assume that all greatness, other than physical strength and dexterity, must be necessarily ethical or intellectual, and be calculated to excite our ethical or intellectual admiration. But let them consider the qualities requisite to produce such results as have just been mentioned, and they will see that no assumption could be more wide of the truth.

A man who should, without underpaying his employees, succeed in manufacturing for the poorer classes boots, jackets, or shirts better in quality and very much less in price than those which they are accustomed to buy now, would probably have to devote a large part of his life to the consideration of a particular kind of seemingly sordid detail. To a man of wide culture and brilliant imagination, the concentration of his faculties on details such as these would be impossible; and if he wished to produce any of the results in question, he would soon discover that he could not. The men who do produce them are rendered capable of doing so, not by the width of their minds, but by the exceptional narrowness. The intellectual stream flows strongly because it is confined in a narrow channel, and thus what to the superficial observer seems a sign of their inferiority, is really, so far as the results are concerned, one of the chief causes of their greatness.

The mean man with the little thing to do

Sees it and does it;

The great man with the great end to pursue

Dies ere he knows it.

Robert Browning very tersely puts the case thus. We have only to alter his language in one respect. Seeing that the results we have now in view are realised results or nothing, the "*mean man*," as an agent of material progress, will be the "great man," and the "great man" will be the little.

So, too, with regard to the man who affects the history of his country by formulating and popularising some particular political demand—the secret of such a man's success, in four cases out of five, will be found to lie in the greatness, not of his intellect, but of his will—in an exceptionally sanguine temperament, in exceptional courage and energy, and very likely in an exaggerated belief in his own nostrums, which, instead of being a sign of great intellectual acuteness, is incompatible with it.

No doubt social progress, as a whole, has required and does require for its production intellectual powers of the highest and rarest kind. The point here insisted on is that it is not produced by intellectual powers alone, and that intellectual powers alone would be quite unable to produce it. Thus the sorrows and disappointments of the unfortunate inventor are proverbial; and the reason is that great inventive powers are frequently accompanied by a very feeble will and a fantastic ignorance of the world; the inventor, though strong as a mind, being pitiably weak as a man. He can do everything with his inventions except make them useful to anybody. He might be practically far greater were he to lose some of his intellectual powers, could he thereby develop some of the humbler qualities in which he is wanting. As it is, he resembles a chronometer which is without a main-spring, and which is useless when compared with a ten-and-sixpenny watch. Hence the inventor has so frequently to ally himself with the man of enterprise, and only becomes great, as a social force, by doing so. Such unions are often sufficiently strange in appearance. We see some man whose intellect is the finest machine imaginable, but he is only redeemed from absolute and grotesque uselessness by his partner, who is little better than an inspired bagman. But such a bagman's gifts, however the inefficient theorist may despise them, are, though less striking than the inventor's, often quite as rare. No doubt many great inventors have the practical gifts as well as the intellectual, and their greatness, in such cases, is comprehended completely in themselves. It remains, however, an equally composite thing, no matter whether it takes two men or only one to complete it; and exceptional intellect is only one of its elements. The other qualities with which it requires to be allied, and which alone give it its practical value, such as determination, shrewdness, and a certain thickness of skin, though often remarkable individually for the exceptional degree to which they are developed, just as often unite to produce practical greatness, not because of the exceptional degree to which they are developed, but of the exceptional proportions in which they are combined. Some of the most essential of them, indeed, need not be exceptional at all, except from the fact of their association with others that are so. Much greatness, for instance, of the most powerful kind, consists mainly of very ordinary sense in conjunction with extraordinary energy; and energy is often, as has already been pointed out, in proportion to the narrowness rather than to the width of the imagination.

Greatness, in short, as an agent of social progress, is in most cases not a single quality, but a peculiar combination of many; its composition varies according to the character of the results in the production of which the great men are severally more efficient than the majority; and it often depends less on the extent to which any special faculty is developed, in comparison with the same faculty as possessed by ordinary men, than it does on the degree to which each faculty is developed as compared with the others possessed by the great man himself.

When we speak of greatness, then, in the sense here attributed to the word—when we speak of great men as agents of social progress—we do not mean that the world is divided into ordinary men and heroes. The members of that minority whom we group together as great men, though some of them are, no doubt, of noble and heroic proportions, are for the most part great in relation to special results only; even in relation to these special results they are great in very various degrees, and many of them in other relations may be ordinary, or even less than ordinary. It must therefore be clearly understood that greatness, as an agent of social progress, is not an absolute thing, and that to say of any one man that he possesses more greatness than another is a statement which, taken by itself, has no definite meaning. When we say that a man is great we mean that he is exceptionally efficient in producing some particular result, which is either implied or specified—that he is great in commanding armies, or in managing hotels, or in conducting public affairs, or in cheapening and improving the manufacture of this or that commodity; and when we say that such and such a man possesses the quality of greatness to such and such a degree we mean that he produces results of a given kind, which are in such and such a degree better or more copious than results of the same kind which are produced by other people.

The inequality of men, then, in natural capacity being an obvious fact, and the nature and the degrees of their inequalities having been now generally explained, we may re-state, with a meaning more precise than was formerly possible, the fundamental proposition implied in the great-man theory, when that theory is raised from a rhetorical to a scientific formula. Progress of an appreciable kind, in any department of social activity and achievement, takes place only when, and in proportion as, some of the men who are working to produce such and such a result are more efficient in relation to that class of result than the majority; or conversely, if a community contained no man with capacities superior to those possessed by the greater number, progress in that community would be so slow as to be practically non-existent.

We must now go on to inquire what is the precise way in which the men who are superior to the majority bring progress about; and we shall find that, however various they may be in other respects, they all promote progress in a way that is fundamentally similar.

# CHAPTER II
## PROGRESS THE RESULT OF A STRUGGLE NOT FOR SURVIVAL, BUT FOR DOMINATION

It has already been explained that the *great man*, as here understood, does not in any way correspond with the *fittest man* in the Darwinian struggle for existence. The fittest man in the Darwinian sense merely promotes progress by the physiological process of reproducing his slight superiorities in his children, and thus raising in the slow course of ages the general level of capacity throughout subsequent generations of his race. The great man, on the contrary, promotes progress, not because he raises the capacity of the generations that come after him, but because he rises individually above the general level of his own. This, however, is only one of the differences by which the great man is distinguished from the fittest. There are two others, of which the first that we must consider is as follows.

The fittest man, or the survivor in the Darwinian struggle for existence, is, so far as his own contemporaries are concerned, greater than his inferiors only in respect of what he accomplishes for himself, or for those immediately dependent on him. He is the man who lives and thrives whilst others die or languish, because whilst they can secure for themselves but little of what is requisite for life and health, he, by his superior gifts, is able to secure much. "*Families*," says Mr. Spencer, "*whom the increasing difficulty of obtaining a living does not stimulate to improvement in production are on the high road to extinction, and must ultimately be supplanted by those whom the difficulty does so stimulate.*" That is to say, Mr. Spencer, and all our modern sociologists with him, conceive of the fittest as a man, or a man and his family, who fight for their food in isolation, like a lion and lioness with their cubs, and who affect their contemporaries only by being better fed than they, or as a race-horse affects its competitors only by being first at the winning post.

But the great man, as an agent of progress, shows his greatness in a way precisely opposite to that in which the fittest man shows his fitness. This it is that our contemporary sociologists all fail to perceive, and endless error is the consequence. The great man, unlike the strongest lion, promotes progress by increasing the food-supply not of himself, but of others; or if he increase his own, as he no doubt generally does, he does so only by showing others how to increase theirs. He is like a lion who should be better fed than the rest of the lions in his region, not because he took a carcase from them for which they all were fighting, but because he showed them how to find others which they never would have found unaided, and took for himself in payment a small portion of each. The great man, in fact, as an agent of social progress, is great not in virtue of any completed results which he produces directly, by the action of his own hands or brains, or which he exhibits in his own person, but in virtue of the completed results which, by some simultaneous influence which he exercises over the brains or hands of others, he enables others to exhibit in themselves, or produce or do in the form of products or social services.

In order to realise this great truth, let us begin with considering that form of greatness which promotes social progress by supplying it with its first materials, and from which all other kinds of greatness draw some portion of their nourishment. It so happens that one of the most remarkable thinkers of this century, who, though he preceded Mr. Spencer, belongs to the same school, is able to assist us here by a very apt and remarkable passage.

John Stuart Mill, in that section of his *System of Logic* to which he gives the title of *"The Logic of the Moral Sciences,"* writes thus. *"In the difficult process of observation and comparison which is required (for the purpose of obtaining a better understanding of the laws of empirical sociology, and especially of social progress) it would evidently be a great assistance if it should happen to be the fact that one element in the complex existence of social man is pre-eminent over all the others, as the prime agent of the social movement. For we could then take the progress of that one element as the central chain, to each successive link of which, the corresponding links of all the other progressions being appended, the succession of facts would by this alone be presented in a kind of spontaneous order, far more approaching to the real order of their filiation than could be obtained by any other merely empirical process. Now the evidence of history and that of human nature combine, by a striking instance of consilience, to show that there really is one social element which is predominant and almost paramount amongst the agents of social progression. This is the state of the speculative faculties, including the nature of the beliefs which by any means they have arrived at, concerning themselves and the world by which they are surrounded. Thus,"* Mill continues, *"to take the most obvious case, the impelling force to most of the improvements effected in the arts of life is the desire for increased material comfort; but as we can only act on external objects in proportion to our knowledge of them, the state of knowledge at any given time is the limit of the industrial improvement possible at that time, and therefore the progress of industry must follow and depend upon the progress of that knowledge."*

Any one who was inclined to be hypercritical might object, and object with justice, that the practical application of knowledge often lags behind the speculative attainment, and that material progress therefore, at certain times, depends on some new state of the practical rather than of the speculative faculties; but apart from this not very important inaccuracy of expression, Mill's way of putting the case is admirable for its lucidity and for its truth; and we may, for our present purpose, be content to take it as it stands. All civilisation depends on the accumulation of speculative knowledge, and all progress in civilisation depends on an increase in speculative knowledge.

Speculative knowledge, however, does not increase of itself. It is not acquired without considerable effort; and people acquire it only because they strongly desire to do so. Such being the case, let us turn to another passage, taken likewise from the writings of Mill, and occurring in the very same chapter as that which has just been quoted. "*It would be a great error,*" says Mill, "*and one very little likely to be committed, to assert that speculation, intellectual activity, the pursuit of truth, is amongst the more powerful propensities of human nature, or holds a predominating place in the lives of any save decidedly exceptional individuals. But notwithstanding the relative weakness of this principle among other sociological agents, its influence is the main determining cause of social progress, all the other dispositions of our nature which contribute to that progress being dependent on it for accomplishing their share of the work.*"

Now what does this passage mean? About its meaning, and the truth of its meaning, there can be no possible doubt; but it will be well to observe the extraordinary confusion in which Mill involves what he means by his perverse manner of expressing it. In the first sentence of this last passage he tells us as clearly as possible that with regard to the pursuit of truth, and the power of discovering and understanding it, mankind are divided broadly into two classes—the great majority with whom the "*pursuit of truth*" and "*intellectual activity*" are "*slight propensities,*" and "*the decidedly exceptional individuals*" with whom these propensities are overmastering. But he has no sooner drawn this clear and all-important distinction between the two classes than he proceeds to undo his own work and mixes them together again in one unmeaning blur. He converts his statement that only "*the decidedly exceptional individuals*" desire truth with any great intensity, and have the faculties requisite for discovering it, into the statement that if we take "*the decidedly exceptional individuals*" and the majority together, and regard them as one body, which he calls "*mankind,*" we shall find that the average desire for truth is lukewarm, and the faculties for discovering it insufficient. He might just as well group Shakespeare with a hundred ordinary men; tell us that Shakespeare could write the greatest poetry the world has ever known, and that the hundred other men could write no poetry at all, and then convert these statements into the following—that the one hundred and one men, Shakespeare included, could only write poetry of a very moderate quality.

This confusion of statement, however, on the part of Mill, is merely mentioned here in passing, as one more example of the nature of that inveterate error—namely the ignoring of the differences between one class of men and another—which has made modern sociology so useless for practical purposes. The sole point which really now concerns us is this. In spite of the verbal, and indeed the mental confusion into which Mill lapses, the truth which he was struggling to express, and which no one, he says, would be likely to contradict, is not that, as he nonsensically puts it, the speculative faculties are weak in mankind generally, but that amongst the larger part of mankind they have hardly any efficiency at all, whilst "*in decidedly exceptional individuals*" they are intense, active, and conquering; and that consequently it is these "*decidedly exceptional individuals*" who practically constitute "*the one social element which is predominant, and almost paramount, amongst the agents of social progression.*"

Now such being the case, let us resume our present inquiry, and ask how do these individuals who alone strongly desire truth, and have the faculties for discovering it, perform the practical part which Mill so rightly assigns to them? By what kind of conduct do they become "*agents of social progression*" so as to raise communities from the level of helpless savagery and gradually endow them with all the resources of civilisation? One thing is perfectly clear. They do not so by the mere act of acquiring knowledge, by laying up this treasure in a napkin, or by showing it secretly to one another. They do so only by diffusing it, in such measure as is practicable, amongst a circle of men much wider than themselves. They do so, that is to say, by influencing the minds of others, by guiding their attention to this and to that fact, by providing, as it were, a go-cart for their weaker intellectual faculties, and compelling them to confront and assent to such and such propositions. All that mass of developing knowledge and expanding ideas which forms not only the basis but a part of all progressive civilisation, and is commonly called by the general name of enlightenment, is produced solely by the influence on average minds of the minds that are "*decidedly exceptional.*" It is not produced by the fact that the "*decidedly exceptional*" minds are stocked with such ideas and with such knowledge themselves, but by the fact that they communicate such a measure of these to average minds as average minds are severally able to receive.

To realise the truth of this we need do no more than consider for a moment the ordinary process of education. The schoolmaster and the college tutor, by the State or some other authority, are compelled to give their pupils instruction in certain subjects. But there is another kind of compulsion involved in the matter also; and this has to do not with the selection of the subjects that are to be taught, but with what is to be taught about them. The general progress of a community depends  primarily upon this; and what is to be taught about them is determined not by the State, or by any other legally constituted body, but by the masters of speculative knowledge, by contemporary men of science, scholars, historians, and philosophers. Knowledge advances because these men are not only adding to it, but because they are perpetually assimilating the new discoveries with the old; and these men, by means of their comments on previous writers, or by new works of their own, often reproduced in the form of text-books, put the word into the teachers' mouths; and the teachers, like the prophet Balaam, are compelled to speak it. In other words, great speculative thinkers are great as agents of mental civilisation and enlightenment only because, and only in so far as, they settle for others what these others shall believe and think.

And now let us pass from mental progress to material—that is to say, from speculative knowledge to applied knowledge; and the truth that is being here insisted on will become clearer still. The master of knowledge, as applied to production, is the inventor. Now the most perfect and important machines ever devised by man—let us say the steam-engine and the printing press—had they been planned by their original inventors in all their present completeness, but kept by the inventors to themselves in the form of working models, made by their own hands and shut up in their own rooms, would have left the arts of life totally unaffected; our fastest means of travelling would still be the stage-coach;  our few books would be produced by the methods of the mediæval scriptorium. These machines are instruments of social progress only because, and in so far as, they are multiplied and brought into use; and they could not be multiplied—as efficient implements, they could not be even made—without the co-operation of an enormous number of workers. It is probable indeed that in constructing the very model itself an inventor will have to employ some labour besides his own. Thus this first and preliminary step towards rendering his apparatus a factor in social progress he can take only by influencing one or two other men, at all events—artisans whose technical action he directs in such a way that it produces something specifically different from anything which it had produced before; and as the apparatus is reproduced on a larger scale, put on the market, multiplied so as to meet a growing demand, and thus actually produces an effect on the arts of life, this practical result takes place only because, and in so far as, the number of artisans whose action is influenced by the inventor increases. The inventor, in other words, is an agent of "*social progression*" only because the particularised knowledge of which his invention consists is embodied either in models, or drawings, or written or spoken orders, and thus affects the technical action of whole classes of other men, just as Mr. Spencer affects, by means of his manuscript, the technical actions of the compositors who put his treatises into type.

Material progress, however, depends not only on the inventor and his machine. It depends also on the uses to which his machine is to be put. Here we shall find a new kind of greatness to be necessary—that which is called business ability; and we shall find that this operates precisely like the greatness of the inventor, through the influence which its possessor exercises over other men.

All progress or development in commerce and in the arts of production is in proportion to the correspondence in every place and season of the goods brought into the market with the contemporary wants of the buyers. If it were not for this correspondence of the economic supply with the demand, progress in production would not be social progress at all; for just as a community does not become materially civilised by the mere act of wanting what it cannot get, so it does not become materially civilised by being presented with what it does not want—clothes, for example, which it could not possibly wear, and books in an unknown language, which it could not possibly read, or diminutive houses and furniture fit only for dolls. Now in any progressive community the wants of the buyers are in constant process not only of development but fluctuation, and are rarely quite the same in any two localities simultaneously. In order, therefore, that what is supplied may be in correspondence with what is wanted, it is necessary that in each industry the nature of the commodities produced be continually modified by men with a special sort of knowledge of the world; and also, since want, in the sense of efficient demand, depends on the price at which these commodities can be supplied, it is necessary, just as it is in the case of the manufacture of machinery, that the army of men whose labour is involved in producing them shall be subject to men who, by their powers of industrial generalship, will be able to reduce the cost of reproduction to a minimum. Every business, in fact, and every industrial enterprise, succeeds or fails, not according to the amount of average labour involved in it, but according to the talents and energy by which this labour is directed. Thus in the economic domain, even more than in the intellectual, the great man is seen to be an agent of "*social progression*," in virtue not of the results which he himself produces by the direct action of his own hands or brain, but of the results which, being what he is, he causes to be produced by others.

And now having dealt with the great man as an agent of speculative progress which, as Mill says, is at the bottom of progress of all other kinds, and having dealt with him also as an agent of that manufacturing, commercial, economic or material progress which Mill cites as the chief example of what practical progress is, and having shown how the essence of his greatness is his power of influencing others, let us illustrate this truth finally by a brief reference to three other kinds of human and social activity which exhibit it in a light so obvious that it requires no explanation. These three kinds of activity are the military, the political, and the religious. The great soldier, as has been said already, is essentially the great commander—the man who makes others act and group themselves in a specific way. The statesman not only aims at benefiting his countrymen generally, but he achieves his aim by the same means as the soldier, namely, by influencing the actions of others in certain specific respects; whilst the man who is socially great in the domain of morals and religion is the man whose teaching and example affect the actions, and even the inmost feelings, of multitudes, or gives precision to their faith.

But here, having reduced to a truism this important truth that the great man, as an agent of social progress, is great only because he is able to exercise a specific influence over others, it is necessary to turn our attention to a different order of facts altogether. Greatness, as we have seen already, is of very many kinds. It is a varying compound of various and variously developed qualities; and its degree is measured by its efficiency in producing this or that result by which society is benefited. But greatness, in the sense of exceptional power of so influencing others that some given result shall be produced by them, has other varieties besides those that have been already mentioned. Each domain of progress has not only its own leaders, but it has leaders who desire to lead men in very different directions. There are scientists with conflicting theories, inventors with rival inventions, statesmen with rival policies. It follows accordingly that though all these men may be possessed of talents indefinitely above the average, they would not all of them, were their influence over other men equal, affect society in an equally advantageous way. Some men, indeed, whose talents are "*decidedly exceptional*" would, on account of some flaw or defect in their character, not promote, but, on the contrary, retard true progress, in exact proportion as they made their views prevail. Thus, though all progress is due to great men, all great men would not promote progress; or they would, at all events, not promote it equally. Progress, therefore, as resulting from the actions of great men, depends on the degree to which certain of them make their own views prevail, and secure the rejection of others which are directly or indirectly opposed to them. It depends, that is to say, on a keen competitive struggle which is continually taking place within the limits of the exceptional minority.

And here we come to that further point of difference, which still remains to be noticed, between the part played in social progress by the great man, and the part in it played by the fittest according to the Darwinian theory. Two points of difference between them have been noted and explained already, one being that the fittest man promotes progress only because he raises, by a physiological process, the average capacities of his successors, whereas the great man promotes progress because he is himself more capable than his contemporaries; the other being that the fittest fulfils his social function by fighting for his own hand, without any reference to others, whereas the great man fulfils his solely by influencing others. We are now coming to a third point, which is, for practical purposes, even more important than the preceding.

The great-man theory, just like the theory of Darwin, involves a competitive struggle. This struggle is a struggle between great men; and its existence is a fact of too obvious a character to have escaped the notice of even the most inaccurate of our social evolutionists. But they one and all of them have completely misunderstood its nature. They have hastened to identify it with the Darwinian struggle for existence, from which it differs in the most vital manner conceivable; and, obscuring it thus by a loose and misleading analogy, they have managed to blind themselves to its entire practical significance. The Darwinian struggle for existence no doubt has its counterpart in the contemporary competition of labourers to find remunerative employment, and in the fact that those who are least successful in finding it would, if left to themselves, be continually dying off. In a progressive country there is, or there always tends to be, a larger number of would-be labourers than there is of tasks which at the moment can be profitably assigned to them. A struggle therefore is involved in obtaining work of any kind; and for the higher kinds of work the struggle is very keen. But this is not the struggle to which modern progress is due. Progress, in the sense of the rapid and appreciable movement which alone concerns us here, is—to confine ourselves for a moment to the domain of industry—not the result of a struggle to execute work in the best way, but is the result of a struggle to give the best orders for its execution. It presupposes the existence of a certain amount of skill; but it does not, except in its very earliest stages, depend on the struggle of so many thousand men, each to become individually a more skilful worker than his fellows. It is, on the contrary, when its earliest stages have been passed, so independent of any further increase of skill in the individual worker, that it continues its course whilst skill remains stationary.

This is shown by the fact that some of the greatest advances ever made in material civilisation have been made during the active lifetime, and with the aid of the hands and muscles, of a single generation of workers, and has implied no improvement at all either in their acquired faculties or their inherited. Let us take, for instance, the introduction of the electric light, and the way in which it is superseding gas. The mechanics first employed to make the appliances for its production were none of them asked to perform any task which required on their part any new knowledge or dexterity. All they were asked to do, and all they did, was to submit their existing faculties to some new external guidance: and the electric light, in so far as it has superseded gas, has superseded it not because it is the product of more skilful labour, but because it is the product of manual labour directed by a set of inventors and employers, who, so far as regards certain social requirements, direct it more successfully than another set. The struggle which it represents is a struggle between employers only. It does not, except by accident, represent any struggle between the employed.

And what is true of the struggle which produces industrial progress, is true of that which produces progress of all other kinds. Scientific knowledge increases in proportion as those exceptional individuals whose studies have brought them most near to the truth are able to fight down the opinions of the exceptional individuals who differ from them, and to impress their own undisputed upon the world. Such knowledge does not increase on account of any struggle amongst the learners, which causes some of them to become more and more apt in learning. It grows on account of a struggle between philosophers, each of whom aims at settling what the learners shall learn. And with regard to religion and politics the case is just the same. The progressive struggle is primarily between rival prophets and politicians. The spread of Christianity, for instance, was not brought about by Christian races exterminating those that were not Christians. It was brought about by Christian thinkers and teachers discrediting the doctrines taught by thinkers and teachers who were opposed to them. Free-trade, again, in this country has not triumphed over protectionism, because the mass of free-traders have exterminated the mass of protectionists. It has triumphed simply because, in the eyes of the majority, one school of theorists has succeeded in discrediting another.

Now these facts, which, when once stated, are so obvious, not only throw the Darwinian struggle for existence altogether into the background as an agent in social progress, but they show that it presents us with no true analogy to that kind of struggle from which progress principally results. They show us, on the contrary, that the struggle which produces social progress, though it resembles the Darwinian struggle in one point, is in all other points contrasted with it. The struggle of one employer against another to direct labour in the most advantageous way, or the struggle of one politician or religious teacher against another to secure for his own views the largest number of adherents, is so far like the Darwinian struggle for existence, that it is a struggle in which individual is pitted against individual, and the gain of the successful is the loss of the unsuccessful. But the limits within which this struggle is confined are very narrow indeed; and the mass of the community takes no part in it whatsoever.

In order to show this with the utmost clearness possible, let us turn again to the domain of economic progress, which generally supplies the sociologist with his simplest and most luminous illustrations. The success of the strongest and ablest employers—that is to say, the heads of the most successful businesses—may involve, and does involve their selection for survival as employers, and does involve the extinction, as employers, though not necessarily as men and parents, of their weaker and less able rivals; but it involves no struggle for existence with the men employed by them—that is to say, with the great masses of the community. Two men, we will say, start rival hotels, and each begins with a staff of a hundred persons. One of the two understands his business far better than the other. His hotel is always full, whilst his rival's is half empty. The latter at last becomes bankrupt; the former buys his business, and together with his premises takes over his staff. He employs two hundred persons, instead of a hundred as at first; the hotel of the bankrupt, which the bankrupt ran at a loss, now yields the same profit as the other; and the aggregate takings of the two are thus increased largely. Here we have a community of two hundred and two persons offering a marked example of great material progress; and this progress has been the result of a genuine struggle for existence. But the struggle for existence has been between two persons only—that is to say, between the two hotel-keepers. As *hotel-keepers* existence is the very thing they have been struggling for, and the survival of the one has meant the disappearance of the other; but between them and the two hundred persons employed by them there has been no struggle at all. The achievement by the successful hotel-keeper of a fortune double that with which he started has not involved any diminution in the wages of his staff. It will, on the contrary, if we are to take the case now in question as typical of the survival of the fittest employers generally, have not only not diminished their wages, but very largely increased them. For here there is one further truth which naturally introduces itself to our observation. Whatever allowance it may be necessary to make for the lowest class or residuum of our modern populations, it is the most clearly proved and prominent fact in modern industrial history—and one which even socialists are now ceasing to deny—that along with the vast increase in wealth which the ablest employers have, by their struggle with rivals, secured for their own enjoyment, there has been not a corresponding diminution, but a corresponding increase in the means of subsistence that have gone to the population generally. The average income per head in this country of that class—composed mainly of wage-earners—which does not pay income tax has, in terms of money, nearly trebled itself during the present century; its purchasing power has increased in a yet larger ratio, and its increase will be found to have been most rapid and striking at periods when the struggle amongst the employing class has been keenest.

It will thus be seen that the struggle which produces economic progress—and progress of every kind is produced in the same way—is not a general struggle which pervades the community as a whole; neither is it a struggle between the majority and an exceptionally able minority, in which both classes are struggling for what only one can win, and in which the gain of the one involves the loss of the other; but it is a struggle which is confined to the members of the minority alone, and in which the majority play no part as antagonists whatsoever. It is not a struggle amongst the community generally to live, but a struggle amongst a small section of the community to lead, to direct, to employ, the majority in the best way; and this struggle is an agent of progress because it tends to result, not in the survival of the fittest man, but in the domination of the greatest man.

# CHAPTER III
## THE MEANS BY WHICH THE GREAT MAN APPLIES HIS GREATNESS TO WEALTH-PRODUCTION

The whole secret of social progress, other than the most rudimentary, is summed up in the formula with which the preceding chapter has concluded. Progress is the result of the domination or the triumphant influence of the greatest. That is to say, the civilisation of the entire community depends alike for its advance and for its maintenance on a struggle which is confined within the limits of an exceptional class; and the ordinary members of the community are connected with it only by the fact that when the fittest competitor achieves the domination for which he is struggling, they, instead of being defeated by him, share the advantage of his victory. When the scientific doctor discredits the theories of the quack, when the competent organiser of industry causes the ruin of the incompetent, when a good ministry drives a bad from office, when a great general supersedes one who is inferior, or when a true religious teacher destroys the influence of a false, the whole community gains, except the men who have personally lost authority, and who share the merited fate of their own errors or deficiencies.

The progress and the maintenance, then, of civilisation in any community depends on its possessing a number of great men, of which number the greatest shall, by competition with the others, succeed in gaining a control over the beliefs and actions of the majority.

Here, however, we are introduced to two new sets of facts, which have not thus far come under our consideration at all.

In the first place, great men do not come into the world ready-made. Their greatness is potential only, or in other words it is practically non-existent, until it has been developed; and the process of developing it is in most cases extremely arduous. The philosopher, the soldier, the inventor, the statesman, the great merchant or manufacturer, achieve success only by prolonged and intense effort, by study, by concentrated thought, by action, by rude experience. Genius, indeed, has been defined as an infinite capacity for taking trouble; and the definition, though very incomplete, is, so far as it goes, true. No one, however, takes trouble without a motive; and a motive being some object of desire, such as money, rank, or pleasure, which a man hopes to attain by a certain line of action, it follows that if a community is to possess great men as actual agents of progress, and not merely as wasted potentialities, its social constitution must be such as to offer and make attainable positions, possessions, pleasures, or other advantages which its potentially great men will feel to be worth working for.

In the second place, since the great man, as we have seen, is an agent of progress and civilisation only because he influences others—because he guides their speculative beliefs, and in certain respects commands their actions—the society or community to which the great man belongs must be such as not only to supply him with a motive for exercising this influence, but also to enable him to secure for himself the means by which it may be exercised; and, furthermore, the means in question must be of a kind which will enable the rival great men to bring their respective capacities to a decisive practical test, so that the influence of the most efficient may establish itself, and that of the less efficient cease.

Now the whole question of motive we will deal with later on. We will for the present put it altogether aside. We will assume a natural impulse on the part of all great men to develop their powers to the utmost, and employ them in influencing others, wholly independent of any other reward than such a minimum of sustenance and comfort as is physically essential to their efficiency; and we will confine our attention altogether to the question of the means by which the influence of the great men over the majority is obtained.

Human progress, however, being a complex thing, and taking place in different domains of activity, the means by which the great man influences others will vary with the nature of the results which his influence aims at eliciting. The social activities on which progress depends, though they may be subdivided indefinitely, are reducible to five kinds—intellectual, religious, military, economic, and political; and with regard to the two first, the influence of the great man exerts itself to determine what others shall believe and think; with regard to the three last, it exerts itself to determine what others shall do.

Now out of these five domains of activity the three first—namely, the intellectual, the religious, and the military—are such that the means by which the great man makes his influence felt in them hardly require discussion. In the first place, they are obvious—

there is no dispute about what they are; and, in the second place, the fact of their being what they are has no bearing, except such as is very remote, on any disputed question concerning the practical organisation of society. In the intellectual world thinkers, scholars, and men of science gain their influence by discussions, for the most part embodied in books, which discussions are carried on before a jury of expert critics, each man defending his own views against the views of those who differ from him; and the jury of experts ultimately gives its verdict, to which sooner or later the community at large submits. The religious leader gains his influence similarly. He gains it by arguments and persuasions, which are felt by a band of followers to touch the spirit more deeply than those of other prophets. He gives to his disciples, and his disciples give to the multitude. But these means are of so universal a kind, and have so little connection with any specific social arrangements, that none of the disputed points of social politics are involved in them; and we consequently have at present no occasion to discuss them. So, too, with regard to the military leader, though the means which are employed by him do, beyond a doubt, imply social arrangements of a very specific kind—namely, an iron system of discipline, with death and the lash to sanction it; yet these arrangements, however they may be denounced by sentimentalists, have always been found essential to the efficiency of every army; and though many worthy people would abolish military activity altogether, and whilst socialists especially express themselves anxious to do so, it is perfectly evident—nor would any socialist deny it—that a socialist State, if it had to fight for its existence, would be obliged to enforce the required military discipline by methods essentially identical with those of Cæsar or Wellington. It may, indeed, be disputed whether the great military leader is not a superfluous figure on the social stage; but so long as his greatness makes itself felt at all, it will continue to make itself felt by the same means.

The only domains of social activity, therefore, in which the means employed by the great man to control the actions of others so that ordinary men may be guided by the faculties of the exceptional— the only domains of activity in which these means, thus employed, really require minute and careful discussion, and have really a direct bearing on the practical problems of the day—are the domain of economic production and the domain of political government. These, indeed, may be said to contain between them the whole of the questions with regard to which parties are divided—with regard to which those who believe that the conditions of civilisation may be indefinitely improved but can never be fundamentally altered, are divided from those who believe them to be capable of indefinite metamorphosis.

This is specially true of the domain of economic production; for it is mainly on account of its connection with the production and distribution of wealth that political government excites so much popular interest and forms the subject of so much vehement controversy. And in every other domain of human activity equally, we shall find that the interests, the endeavours, and the disputes of men have an economic process as their basis, or economic progress as their object. The processes of production and commerce are, in fact, the central processes of every nation's life. Government exists to foster them, and changes its form as these processes develop; whilst fleets and armies exist mainly for their protection, and more and more depend on the progress that takes place in them. It is, in short, in the domain of economics that all the social problems of the day either begin or end; and consequently in examining the means by which the great man influences others, the question which it is really our first concern to examine relates to the means by which great men, whose greatness consists in the fact that they are exceptional in their powers of causing the production of wealth, and on whom consequently the wealth of the whole community depends, obtain a control over other men's productive actions.

This control can be secured in two ways only, or else in some way that is a combination or modification of both. One of these ways is slavery; the other is the capitalistic wage-system. Let us consider how the two resemble each other, and also how they differ.

They resemble each other because both, in so far as they subserve progress, subserve it for precisely the same reason. They are both contrivances by which the superior few may secure, so far as industry is concerned, the implicit obedience of the many. On the private lives of the many their effects will be widely different; but so far as concerns their direct connection with industry—their operation on men during the actual processes of production— slavery and the capitalistic wage-system differ only in this: that the one secures the required industrial obedience by operating on men's fears; the other secures it by operating on their desires and wills. Thus the slaves who built the pyramids had each some specified task—the making of so many bricks, the cutting of such and such stones, or the fixing of bricks and stones in such and such situations—which had to be performed if the pyramids were to be built at all. So, too, if the Hotel Metropole at Brighton was to be built at all, the bricklayers, masons, and other workmen who built it had to perform tasks of a precisely similar kind. But obedience to orders on the part of the Egyptian slave was secured by the knowledge on his part that disobedience would be punished by some form of chastisement, and very likely of torture, whilst obedience on the part of the Brighton workman was secured by the knowledge on his part that, unless he chose to yield it, one way, at all events, of earning a livelihood would be closed to him.

It is this latter method of securing industrial obedience that is made possible by the capitalistic wage-system; and it is primarily for this reason that what is called capitalism is an agent of progress, and has developed itself in progressive communities. As for capital itself, this, as we all know, performs part of its functions by assuming the form of machinery, buildings, bridges, railways, and a variety of structures and appliances which are grouped together under the general head of *fixed capital* by economists. But these structures and appliances are themselves the result of the previous influence of great men on the industrial actions of the many; and as it was by means of wage-capital that this influence was secured, the primary and most essential functions which capital fulfils, and which really form the essence of the capitalistic system, are to be found by considering capital as employed in the payment of wages.

Now capital as thus employed consists of an accumulation of the necessaries and comforts of life, by the consumption and use of which men are able to sustain themselves when engaged on works requiring a long period for their completion, which will when completed be useful and produce much, but which, until they are completed, will be of no use at all, and will consequently supply nothing to the workers when actually engaged on them. The simplest example of work of this kind is agriculture. The first man who saved sufficient food to support himself, whilst tilling the soil and waiting for his crops to ripen, was the first capitalist. But capital, when it takes the form of accumulated necessaries and comforts, though it now reaches the workers in the form of wages usually, need not do so of necessity. It need not do so when the work is extremely simple and the methods employed are rude. Wherever agriculture, for example, is in its earliest stages, every husbandman may be his own capitalist, and start with an accumulation of food in his own cottage which will keep him alive till his crops are ready for sale or for consumption. In cases such as these we have capital which, so far as its substance is concerned, is identical with wage-capital, but is not wage-capital nevertheless. In order to turn it into wage-capital it is necessary that these accumulations of food shall pass out of the control of the workers—such as the husbandmen just referred to—and be brought under the control of some other person or persons, who will dole them out to the workers on certain conditions only. The wage-system, in short, does not represent capital as such. It represents capital, in the form of the immediate means of subsistence, as owned or controlled by a small number of persons; and its efficiency as a productive agent resides in the bargain which it enables any great man possessing it to make with ordinary workers—a bargain, not that they shall work such and such a number of hours (for that they would have to do were each man his own employer), but that they shall do their work in accordance with the great man's directions.

Now this fact that the wage-system represents the control of capital by the few—and this is its essential characteristic—is the fact on which, more than on any other, the socialistic opponents of the modern wage-system insist. They are never weary of insisting that it has its foundation in a monopoly. But though they perceive the fact, they entirely miss its significance. Karl Marx conceives of the capitalists as a body of men who, so far as production is concerned, are absolutely inert and passive. Owing to a variety of causes, he says, during the past four hundred years all the means of production have come under their control, and access can be had to them only, as it were, through gates, of which these tyrants hold the key. Outside are the manual labourers, who are the sole producers of wealth, but who, without the means of production, naturally can produce nothing—not even enough to live on; and the sole economic function which the capitalist fulfils is to let the labourers in every day through the gates, on the condition that every evening the unhappy men render up to him the whole produce of their labours, except that insignificant fraction of it which is just necessary to fit them for the labours of the day following. Now it is no doubt theoretically possible that a society might exist, composed of a mass of undifferentiated and undirected manual labourers on the one hand, and on the other of a few passive monopolists who extracted from them most of what they produced, as the price of allowing them the opportunity of producing anything; but it is perfectly certain that a society of this kind would exhibit none of the increasing productive power which, as even Marx and his school admit, is one of the most distinctive features of industry under the capitalistic wage-system. Under that system productive power has increased, not because capital has enabled a few men to remain idle, but because it has enabled a few men to apply, with the most constant and intense effort, their intellectual faculties to industry in its minutest details. It has increased not because the monopoly of capital has enabled the few to say to the many, "We will allow you to work at nothing, unless you give us most of what you produce," but because it has enabled them to say to the many, "We will allow you to work at nothing, unless you will consent to work in the ways that we indicate to you."

The few, so far as our present argument is concerned, may appropriate much of the gross product or little; or they may leave the whole of it to be divided amongst their employees. What they actually have done, or do, or may do, in this respect, is another question altogether, and will be discussed hereafter separately. The essence of the wage-system, in so far as it has influenced the actual processes of production, is in the power it gives to the few to direct the producers, not in the power it gives them to appropriate the products. It will indeed require very little reflection to show us that if the great men in the industrial world would only develop and use their faculties, without any motive of ambition or self-interest to stimulate them,—as indeed at the present moment we are assuming that they do,—they could use the wage-system for the purpose of directing industry merely by monopolising the control of capital without monopolising, and even without sharing in, its possession.

This truth will become plainer still when we reflect that if only certain conditions prevailed which in many civilised countries survived till quite recently, the whole process of production as we now have it might be carried on without any wage-capital at all. These conditions are those of the *corvée* system, under which peasants and others who owned the lands upon which they lived, and maintained themselves on those lands in a certain position of independence, were compelled to place their labour, for so many days a week, at the absolute disposal of this or that superior. Such a system, if applied to modern industry, would have, no doubt, many incidental disadvantages; but if only a number of independent peasant-proprietors could be forced to give half their time to the proprietor of a neighbouring factory, and during that time to work in it under his orders, the entire use and necessity of wage-capital would in theory, at all events, be gone. The same thing is also true of slavery, between which and the wage-system the *corvée* system stands midway. Like the peasant-proprietor, who is forced to give part of his labour to his over-lord, the slave is supplied with the necessaries of life independently of his obedience to the detailed orders of his task-master. The peasant maintains himself by tilling his own fields; the slave-owner feeds his slave just as he would feed an animal. In neither case is the giving or the withholding of a livelihood used as the motive or sanction by which industrial obedience is ensured. Obedience is ensured by the direct application of force, or the knowledge on the slave's part or the peasant's that force will be applied if necessary.

It will, no doubt, be urged by some that whatever assistance is afforded by the talents of the few to the industrial efforts of the many, may be secured by a third means, which is neither slavery nor yet the wage-system—that is to say, by what is called the system of "co-operation." Co-operative production, however, when it differs in anything except in name from production as carried on under the ordinary wage-system, differs from it only in being the wage-system under a thin disguise. For the ideal cooperative factory is simply a factory in which all the shareholders are workers, and all the workers are shareholders, and in which, being shareholders, they elect their manager. Under such conditions, each of these working shareholders may receive his remuneration under the form, not of wages, but of profits. But if any shareholder, or any group of shareholders, should systematically shirk working, or disobey the manager's orders, the whole, or a part of the payment that would be otherwise due to him, would be withheld; for unless some regulation of this kind were in force, it would be impossible to ensure any co-operation amongst the co-operators, or any order, or any equality of diligence. Each worker's profits, then, are in reality his wages, being essentially a payment which is made to him only on condition that he performs certain specified tasks in a certain specified way.

We are thus brought back to the point from which we started—namely, that there are two methods only by which, in the domain of industry, the superior faculties of the few can direct the faculties of the many: firstly, the capitalistic wage-system, which is the method of inducement; secondly, slavery, complete or partial, which is the method of coercion. And of the truth of this assertion the reader shall now be presented with a highly interesting and curiously conclusive proof, taken from the very last quarter in which he would naturally expect to find it. This proof is afforded us by the schemes which, with ever-increasing clearness, have of recent years been put forward by all the more thoughtful socialists.

These enthusiasts, who are still careful to tell us that they regard the wage-system as the source of all social evils, have been slowly coming to perceive that the ability with which the labour is directed is as important a factor in production as the labour itself, which is directed by it. They propose accordingly to regenerate the human race by transferring the ownership of capital from private employers, not to groups of factory-hands, as the "co-operators" propose, but to the State; and by substituting for the private employers a hierarchy of State officials. Now these officials, so far as the wage-system is concerned, if they differed at all from private employers of to-day, would and could differ from them in the following way only. The present dispensers of wages assign the means of subsistence to each worker in proportion to the exactness, intelligence, and efficiency with which he obeys orders. The dispensers of wages under socialism would dispense these means daily to every worker alike, with no immediate reference to his industrial actions whatsoever; and the direction of his actions would be a second, and wholly distinct process.

That such is the case is shown, and indeed distinctly admitted, in a preface to the American edition of *Fabian Essays*. It is there stated that with regard to the apportionment of the means of subsistence, the only *"truly socialistic"* scheme is one which would *"absolutely abolish"* all economic distinctions, *"and the possibility of their again arising, by making an equal provision for the maintenance of all an incident and an indefeasible condition of citizenship, without any regard whatever to the relative specific services of different citizens. The rendering of such services, on the other hand, instead of being left to the option of the citizen, with the alternative of starvation, would be required under one uniform law or civic duty, precisely like other forms of taxation or military service."*

Such, then, is the most advanced socialistic programme—the programme of the men who have set themselves to devise an escape from capitalism. An escape from capitalism it may be; but it is an escape into complete slavery. For the very essence of the position of the slave, as contrasted with the wage-labourer, so far as the direction of his productive actions is concerned, is that he has not to work as he is bidden in order to gain his livelihood, but that, his livelihood being assured to him, he has to work as he is bidden in order that he may avoid the lash, or some other form of punishment; and amongst all the more thoughtful socialists there is now a consensus of admission that the socialistic State would necessarily have in reserve the severest pains and penalties for the idle and the careless and the disobedient.

Since, then—let us once more repeat it—the progress and maintenance of economic civilisation depend, as even socialists are now beginning to perceive, on the industrial actions of average men being subjected to the control of exceptional men, and since this control can be secured by two methods only—that of the wage-payer and that of the slave-owner—it is evident that all progress and civilisation implies the existence of either one system or the other, and that socialists accordingly, in proportion as they reject the wage-system, are obliged to replace it by what is essentially the system of slavery.

We have thus far, however, dealt with but one half of our subject. We have considered merely the means by which any one great man exercises industrial control over the actions of a number of ordinary men. We have still to consider the means by which the most efficient of the great men get this control into their own hands, and take it out of the hands of the less efficient.

Under the *régime* of private capitalism this process is simple. The fitness or efficiency of each great man is according to the acceptability to the public of the goods or services which he offers them. If the public are not pleased with these goods and services, they do not buy or demand them; and the capital of the man by whom they are offered, not being renewed by any money received, melts in his hands, and with it his control over other men's labour. Meanwhile, by a converse process, the great men who offer goods and services which the public desire and find serviceable, renew and increase by their payments the capital which has been disbursed by him, and renew and increase his control over other men's labour along with it.

Now if the wage-system is the sole alternative to slavery as a means by which the great man controls the actions of the ordinary man, it is still more obviously the sole alternative to slavery as a means by which one great man, in controlling them, shall compete against another great man. Indeed, we may speak still more strongly. We may say not only that it is the sole alternative means, but that it is the sole efficient means. And if we desire a proof of this, all we have to do is to repeat our former procedure, and consider how the socialists propose to supply its place.

It is, no doubt, true that when we first begin this consideration it does not appear that we should derive from it much direct enlightenment; because, if we may go by what the socialists themselves tell us, one of their principal objects is to abolish competition altogether. Their protestations, however, with regard to this matter betray a most curious and most amusing confusion of thought. They declare that competition must be abolished because it inflicts misery on the majority—that is to say, on the weakest in what they call the "*cut-throat struggle.*" But, as was shown at great length in the last chapter, competition means two, and two absolutely distinct things—one being a struggle to live, the other a struggle to dominate; and the effects of the two on the majority are altogether different. To this fundamental truth the socialists are completely blind. The struggle to live, or, in other words, the struggle to secure employment, no doubt, when it is severe, does entail suffering on the strugglers. But this struggle, though it often accompanies progress, under the capitalistic system is not essential to it—as is shown by the fact that when such progress is most rapid the struggle in question tends to disappear altogether; for the competition is then amongst the employers to find labour, rather than amongst the labourers to find employment. Now if the struggle for employment could be obviated by any kind of social reform, an indubitable benefit would, no doubt, be conferred on the workers generally. But just as this struggle for work or for existence—this struggle of one worker against another—is not essential to the capitalistic wage-system, and certainly did not originate with it, and just as that system would not necessarily be abolished by its overthrow, so it is not the kind of competition against which the socialists direct their main attacks. Their main attacks are directed against the struggle between the wage-payers, not the wage-earners—that is to say, against the struggle not for existence, but for domination; and the struggle for domination has on the workers generally no evil effects at all, except such as are occasional and accidental. On the contrary, the workers are as much interested in its maintenance as anybody; for not only does it inflict no injury on themselves, but to it that progress in the processes of production is due on which their own hopes depend, as much as do those of their employers. Accordingly, the socialists, profound thinkers as they are, propose to abolish the competition by which the workers benefit, because they confuse it with the competition by which the workers suffer. The point, however, which concerns us here is not that they have made a blunder as to the kind of competition which they should attack, but that the kind of competition which they declare themselves pledged to abolish, as a thing accursed, and the root of all social evils, they really reintroduce into their own programme, altered only by being associated with the system of slavery, and by being robbed of its practical efficiency, and robbed of nothing else.

For our contemporary socialists, who have at last come to perceive that the productivity of labour depends on the ability with which it is directed, perceive also the fact that, out of many possible directors, some would direct it far more efficiently than others. They also perceive the fact that the directors of labour, who, according to their proposals, would be officials of the bureaucratic State, could prove their efficiency only by practical experiment. Now if all capital were, as socialists propose it should be, owned by the State, and if all the means of subsistence were apportioned amongst the citizens equally, without reference to the work performed by them; and if all the directors of labour, whether inventors or business organisers, had to act as State officials, or else not act at all, the practical experiments necessary to show which officials were the fittest could be brought about only by the State investing such and such of them with a quasi-military power over so many regiments of labourers for such and such a time, which power would be renewed if they could persuade the State to reappoint them, or taken from them if the State should be persuaded that some other men, their rivals, would employ this power more usefully. And this is precisely what the proposals of the socialists come to. The whole multitude of State officials who would direct socialistic industry would, according to every socialistic programme, be appointed, promoted, or degraded to the ranks of ordinary workers in accordance with the efficiency shown by them in the practical command of labour. Some socialists propose that these officials should owe their appointment to a central governing body; others propose that they should owe them to popular election; but in either case, appointment, promotion, or degradation would necessarily and avowedly, if it did not depend on favouritism, depend on the practical results which the different men in question elicited from labour by their different methods of directing it. In other words, the whole system of socialistic production would involve and depend on competition; and the only essential difference between this bureaucratic competition under socialism and the competition of capitalists which socialists so furiously denounce, is that whilst the capitalists obtain control over labour by means of wages, which control, by a natural and automatic process, is gradually extinguished unless it is used efficiently, the competitors for office under socialism would obtain the same control by compulsory powers with which the State would invest them, and which they would lose or retain at the pleasure of some more or less arbitrary authority.

Competition, then, between the directors of labour—or, as it is here defined, the struggle for industrial domination—is as much a part of the theoretical *régime* of socialism as it is a part of the actual *régime* of capitalism. The only differences between the two consist, firstly, in the means by which labour is directed, coercion being employed in one case, and in the other the inducement of wages; and, secondly, in the means by which the fittest director is placed in power, and the less fit deprived of it—an official body deciding the matter in the one case, and the mass of the consuming public deciding it in the other for themselves.

Now we may safely say that the *régime* of industrial coercion, or slavery, even though it should bear the name of socialism, is not in these days possible. It is impossible for two reasons—one, that it is out of harmony with the sentiments of the modern world; and the other—equally strong, though not so generally avowed—that it is an exceedingly clumsy and wasteful instrument of competition. We may, accordingly, dismiss it from our consideration; and such being the case, there remains for us the absolute certainty that if society is to make any further industrial advance, or if it is to save itself from a relapse into industrial helplessness, the capitalistic wage-system, and with it capitalistic competition, or, in other words, the competitive struggle for domination, must both of them be continued under some form or other; nor, although they may be modified in an indefinite number of their details, is there any apparent possibility of ever modifying them in any of their essentials. Indeed, the great moral to be drawn from the facts that have been here elucidated is that if any one institution in the modern world threatens to be permanent, that institution is the capitalistic wage-system; and all proposed alterations in it we may set down as impossible in precise proportion as the socialists attach value to them. The foolish dreamers who imagine that they can overthrow it, consider only its outer aspect, and not the forces of which it is the expression. It is perfectly true that this system might at any given time, and in any given country, be paralysed or reduced to ashes; but the forces that would overthrow it would be essentially non-productive. The men who destroyed it would find themselves powerless without it, and would be obliged to submit to, and assist in, its reconstruction. For the outer form of capitalism is not what capitalism is, any more than a painter's brush is the power that paints great pictures. Capitalism, in its essence, is merely the realised process of the more efficient members of the human race controlling and guiding the less efficient; capitalistic competition is the means by which, out of these more efficient members, society itself selects those who serve it best; and no society which intends to remain civilised, and is not prepared to return to the direct coercion of slavery, can escape from competition and the wage-system, under some form or other, any more than it can stand in its own shadow.

With regard, then, to economic production, which, of all social activities, is for the practical sociologist incomparably the most important, what we have thus far seen is as follows. We have seen, not that it is impossible—for this question has been expressly postponed—that men may be made far more equal than they are now in respect of the possession of wealth; but that whatever degree of equality they may some day attain to in its possession, they can never be otherwise than unequal in the parts played by them in its production; that their inequality in productive power is of such a kind as to render the industrial obedience of the larger number of them to the minority the primary and permanent condition on which economic progress is possible; that what feather-brained fanatics call "*economic freedom*" would be merely another name for economic helplessness; and that all the democratic formulas which for the past hundred years have represented the employed as the producers of wealth, and the capitalistic employers as the appropriators of it, are, instead of being, as they claim to be, the expressions of a profound truth, related to truth only as being direct inversions of it. Whatever appearances may seem to show to the contrary, it is the few and not the many who, in the domain of economic production, are essentially and permanently the chief repositories of power. That this is so in the domain of intellect we have seen already. We will now turn our attention to the domain of political government, and consider the part played by the exceptional few there—the nature and origin of their power, and the means by which it is exercised.

# CHAPTER IV
## THE MEANS BY WHICH THE GREAT MAN
## ACQUIRES POWER IN POLITICS

In discussing, with reference to political government, the means by
which the great man controls the actions of others, it will be found
that the point on which we shall have to concentrate our attention
differs somewhat from that which engaged it when we were
discussing the same question with reference to economic
production. For all the points which, with reference to the directors
of industry, it was necessary to establish in opposition to the
sociological sophistries of to-day are, with reference to the political
governor, admitted by all alike. Thus we shall find on reflection
that the extremest democratic reformer, no less than the aristocrat
or the strict upholder of autocracy, admits, firstly, that satisfactory
governors must be exceptional or great men; secondly, that the
fittest great men can be secured by competition only; and, thirdly,
that however they are appointed, and whatever may be the
principles on which they govern, their orders must in every case be
enforced by virtually the same  sanctions. The last of these three
facts—namely, that the commands of the governor must be
enforced by some system of restraint and punishment for the
disobedient—is sufficiently plain to require no further notice; but
the two others, obvious as they really are, are not perhaps generally
realised, and it will be well to give a few words to them.

That the efficient governor, though he need not always be a genius,
must in some respects, at all events, be a great or exceptional man,
is of course admitted by the advocates of autocracy, aristocracy, or
oligarchy. All that requires to be shown is that it is admitted also by
the thinkers who are most opposed to them—by socialists and
extreme democrats. This admission on their part is implied in the
notorious importance attached by them to the machinery of
popular election; for popular election is simply an elaborate means
of expressing the opinion of the people that out of so many
possible governors, this one or that one is endowed with greater
capacity than the others. If the capacities of all were equal, or if
exceptional capacity was not required, the *personnel* of the
government might be chosen by casting lots. Next, as to the
question of competition, it must be obvious to every one that the
popular election of governors is not only an admission that some
few men out of many are greater or more capable than the rest, but

is also, on the part of the candidates for election themselves, competition in one of its intensest and most sharply accentuated forms.

Competition, indeed, is implicit in every form of government. Were it absent in any, it would be absent in complete autocracies; but even in these it is latent, and always ready to come into operation; for the most absolute autocrat, if he happen to make his rule sufficiently odious to a sufficient number of his subjects,— *"postquam cerdonibus esse timendus cœperat"*—will, as history shows us, be assassinated or got rid of somehow, and some other candidate for power, probably an autocrat also, will be put in his place, and will either retain or lose it, according as experiment shows him to be a tolerable ruler, or the reverse. Here is political competition in its most rudimentary form; but it is competition none the less; and it generally involves a competition more advanced than itself; for the most absolute autocrat is obliged to govern through ministers; and these rise and fall according as experiment shows them to be fitter or less fit for the accomplishment of their master's purposes. If, then, even the power of the autocrat rests ultimately on competition and practical experiment, much more does the power of government, under aristocratic and oligarchic constitutions. Oligarchies invariably aim at ruling through their strongest members; and which are the strongest is shown by experimental competition only; whilst political democracy, under all its forms, is experimental competition open and undisguised. A Gladstone remains in power because, as his years of office succeed each other, he satisfies the majority by the manner in which he governs them; and his power is taken from him when the majority cease to be satisfied, not only because they are of opinion that he governs badly, but because they are of opinion that a Disraeli will govern better. A democracy, in fact, and an oligarchy, so far as competition is concerned, differ merely in the way in which the competitors are admitted to the arena, and in the number and character of the jury which awards the prizes.

Since, then, with regard to the points just dealt with—namely, the necessity for great men as governors, for the selection of the fittest of them by competition, and for the use of coercion and punishment as a means of enforcing orders—there is no essential difference between the most extreme democracy and its opposites, in what does that practical or theoretical difference between them consist, by which most undoubtedly the former is distinguished from the latter? The only essential point of difference between them lies, not in their respective schemes or theories of the machinery of government, or of their methods of electing governors, but in their theory of the powers which election communicates to those elected. An elected governor, whether chosen from a large or a small class, is, according to the aristocratic or oligarchic theory, chosen because he is personally wiser than those who elect him; and it is theoretically his mission, within very wide limits, to follow his own judgment, not that of the electors. The democratic theory is the very reverse of this. The elected governor, according to that theory, is elected not because he is supposed to be wiser than his constituents, but because he is supposed to be exceptionally capable of understanding their precise wishes, and giving effect to each of them. In the first of these two cases the governor is like the physician whom the patient calls in, but whose orders he never thinks of disputing. In the second, he is like the professional Spanish letter-writer, whom the illiterate lover employs to put his passion for him grammatically upon paper.

The only point, then, in which democracy can claim to differ essentially, not only from autocracy, but from any form of oligarchy, lies not in its form of government, but in the power that is behind its government. This power, according to democratic theorists, is the power of the mass of ordinary men, as definitely opposed to exceptional men; and the exceptional men who are picked out as governors would necessarily, in an ideal democracy, be exceptional only for such qualities as practical activity and a quick apprehension of the wishes of other people, which would enable them to do what their many-headed master bade them; but they would have to be wanting in any strength of mind or originality which might prompt them to acts out of harmony with their master's temper at the moment, or what is the same thing, to any acts beyond their master's comprehension, even although such acts might be for his future benefit. This is what the democratic theory, in its last analysis, means. All exceptional will is to be smothered or over-ridden by the average will, as is expressed clearly enough in the well-worn democratic formula—every man's vote is to count for one in government; no man's vote is to count for more than one.

Now this theory of the relation of the great man to the many, so far as regards the conduct of civil government, is identical with the theory which, with a much wider application, Mr. Herbert Spencer enunciates as the foundation of his sociological system. As enunciated by Mr. Spencer we have already submitted it to examination, and we have shown that, in every practical sense, it is altogether fallacious, and that its acceptance renders all practical sociology impossible. We will now proceed to show that, as applied even to the most popular forms of government, it is as false as it is when applied to social phenomena generally.

That the essential principle of democracy, as just described, according to which the brain of the ideal ruler is merely a balance for weighing the wills of multitudes, which are dropped into one or other of its scales, like marbles—that this principle has ever yet been completely realised, no democrat will perhaps venture to maintain; but the whole democratic propagandism of the present day implies, before all things else, that its complete realisation is possible, and that every day "the peoples" are getting nearer to it. The facts, however, which are supposed to warrant this conclusion are to be sought, not in the sphere of official government, but without it. They are to be sought not in the conduct of elected legislators, but in the machinery by which they are elected, and, above all, in those unofficial movements, meetings, and agitations by which the prophets of democracy affirm that the great mass of the people is learning to exert the power which was always latent in it, and to express its will with regard to every question of government as it arises, even if it has something yet to learn in the art of securing that its governors shall carry out its commands. It is this view of the situation which is expressed in the popular saying that a constituency has elected a member, or that the people has elected a parliament, with what is called a "mandate" to do some specified thing or things—to break up the United Kingdom, to disestablish the English Church, to penalise the drinking of a glass of beer on Sundays, or to deprive our soldiers of protection against the most malignant of contagious maladies.

Now the democrats, it must be admitted, are so far right, that a real political power has come into existence which has no constitutional connection with the men who nominally govern; and this is frequently used with such efficiency, and with such definite purpose, that official governors—men of most exceptional intellect—are compelled by it to use their intellect for ends which they themselves condemn. Here, then, in this external power, is to be found, if it is to be found anywhere, the will of the many, as conceived of by the theorists of democracy, exerting itself independently of any separate will of the few, and turning the powers of the few into its willing or unwilling instruments.

Now perhaps the question which will in this place most naturally suggest itself is whether this will of the many, however effectively it may be exercised, is really a power that makes for civilisation and progress, and whether it is not more likely to bring harm than benefit to those very collections of ordinary men who exercise it. And this question is, no doubt, extremely pertinent; but it is not one that need engage our attention now. The fact which alone we are now concerned to demonstrate is that the alleged will of the many is not what democrats conceive it to be, and that it is not really the will of the many at all.

For although there is much in the history of the present century to warrant the assumption that the political will of the many is at last emerging as a supreme and independent governing power, we shall find that these movements and opinions, which seem, when viewed superficially, to result from the spontaneous actions and spontaneous thoughts of the many, really imply the influence of exceptional men, just as much as those movements which are avowedly aristocratic in origin; and that in the absence of these men the movements could never have taken place, nor the opinions have ever assumed any uniform and coherent shape.

To understand how this is, we need merely reflect upon the fact that masses of men, as masses, can only have a will at all when their judgments with regard to certain particular questions happen to be absolutely identical, and have thus a cumulative force, like that of weights piled on one another above some substance which it is desired to compress. Now, whatever may be the thoughts, wishes, or opinions which spontaneously shape themselves in the minds of any body of ordinary men—men various in training and temperament, and none of them remarkable for wisdom—these never take a shape which will give them any cumulative power unless amongst the ordinary men there is some man more active than the rest, who weighs them, compares them, eliminates what he thinks to be their discrepancies, adds what is in his opinion necessary to their logical completion, and clothes them in catching language, which appeals both to the mind and to the memory. Not till this is done do the mass of persons concerned realise how identical their opinions on a given question are; and they then perceive them to be identical for an exceedingly simple reason— that the exceptional man has made a mould for them, into which they have all been run.

It is then, for the first time, that the mass of ordinary men become conscious of corporate power; for then they become, with regard to a given question, conscious for the first time that their opinions are absolutely identical, and that in a certain given direction their power is consequently cumulative. But the opinion of these men, whose numbers give political force to it, is very far from representing the capacities of these men only. It represents the capacities, the character, and very probably the personal designs of the exceptional man who supplied that common mould to which the unanimity of the other men's opinions is due; and the one opinion which thus comes to be held by all of them will not be precisely the opinion that was originally held by any. The original opinion of each will have undergone some modification. It will have been softened, emphasised, developed, or other elements will have been added to it, which would never have entered the mind of the ordinary man naturally, and which even when admitted he does but imperfectly understand. Thus whilst a political opinion expressed, or a political demand made, by a body of ordinary men thus absolutely unanimous seems at first sight a genuine expression of the will and the capacities of the many, it always in part, and it very often mainly represents capacities and purposes belonging to one man alone, the many being practically little more than a phonograph, which repeats his words to the world through an enormous resonator.

Let us take, for instance, the two questions of Free Trade and Bimetallism. If any British Government were to revert to the system of protection, it cannot be doubted that throughout the country there would be meetings and demonstrations, at which every throat would be unanimous in shouting condemnation of their conduct. America has witnessed a precisely similar outburst in favour of a proposal to remonetise silver. The issues raised, however, both by the free traders and the bimetallists, are of a kind so complicated that exceedingly few people would be able even to describe their nature clearly enough to satisfy the most lenient examiner who should set them a paper in economics. The majority of those who declared for bimetallism in America had as little to do with forming their own opinions as the little boys would have in a preparatory school who should shout their approval of some new emendation made by one of their masters of a corrupt passage in Pindar; nor does that British opinion in favour of free trade principles which has caused our Government to adopt them, and would hinder or prevent their repudiation, rest in the minds of the majority of those who hold it, on any larger amount of original thought or knowledge. Ninety-nine free traders out of a hundred would never have been free traders at all if it had not been for the oratory of Cobden. The least-educated portion of the citizens of the United States would never have howled themselves hoarse over an intricate financial problem if it had not been for the oratory and the singular activity of Mr. Bryan. Indeed, what is oratory itself, which in all democracies, from that of Athens downwards, has been essential to the work of government, but an embodied expression of the fact that the many are powerless, unless here and there some thinker will think for them, and give them opinions which may form a mould or a nucleus for their own? Even a village meeting is never got together without the agency of some one who is slightly more efficient than the rest. He need not be wiser than they. He very frequently is not; but he has some gift or other which qualifies him for taking the lead. His temperament is more active, his words flow more freely, or he is hampered by less insight into his own ignorance or imbecility; and his opinions are the nucleus round which those of the rest form themselves, and which generally imparts to them something of its own character, as a vinegar plant does to the liquor in which it is immersed.

Without some such nuclei afforded to the many by the few, popular thought is nebulous, and popular will unborn. An exceptional few are essential even to those revolutionary movements which have the destruction of the power of the few for their object. It is impossible for the many to attack one set of superiors, except by submitting themselves to the leadership or dictatorship of another set; and although these last may to a certain extent represent the multitude, it is usually just as true that the multitude represent them. The multitude cannot even unite to influence those exceptional persons to whom is entrusted the official work of government without placing themselves under the influence of another set of exceptional persons; and thus the extremest democracy will be found, if we only look below the surface, to be neither more nor less than an oligarchy disguised. It is, no doubt, true that those who actually govern do in a certain sense derive their power from the many. They do so even in countries where the supreme governor is an autocrat. In countries with a popular constitution they derive their power from the many by an organised and conscious system; but even in the extremest democracies the average men can exercise their power only by constant processes of surrendering it into the hands of exceptional men. They surrender it into the hands of the exceptional men for the simple and enduring reason that, with very few exceptions, which will be examined in another place, it comes into existence only in the very act of surrendering it; and the many accordingly place themselves in the hands of the few because, from the very constitution of human nature, they cannot avoid doing so.

We thus see that even in that sphere of political action in which, if anywhere, the many should be independent of the few, the many without the few would have no power at all.

The apologists of democracy, however, have another argument left them. They may contend that the exceptional men, who are necessary to the development of the collective powers of ordinary men, though each of them is constantly, with regard to particular questions, following his own devices rather than the instructions of the electorate, do on the whole, and in the long-run, substantially carry out the intentions and devices of those who are theoretically their masters; and that though they may do what their masters could never have thought of for themselves, yet they can never continue to do anything of which their masters do not actually approve. Now even were this representation of the case true, it would leave untouched that broad and fundamental truth on which it is the primary purpose of the present work to insist. It would leave untouched the truth that the great mass of human beings are helpless without the assistance of a minority more efficient than themselves. If ninety-nine average men, through the aid of a hundredth man who is exceptional, can develop and give effect to a collective will, which is altogether their own, and originates entirely with themselves, but if they can neither develop it nor give effect to it unless the hundredth man lent them his services, the power of this one man is as essential to the power of the ninety-nine, as it would be if the orders which he executes had been largely originated by himself; just as a lens is essential to the photographer's camera though its function is solely to focalise, not to colour, the rays transmitted by it. Accordingly, even on the above hypothesis, the modern democratic formula, which makes each man count for one, and nobody count for more than one, would, if judged scientifically, be absolutely and fundamentally false; for the power ascribed by it to the accumulated faculties of equals would be really the power of equals united with the power of a superior; and the difference between the equals and the superior would be at once apparent from this—that if one of the equals were subtracted, the power of the whole hundred would be diminished by one ninety-ninth only; but if the one superior were subtracted, it would collapse altogether. Thus the presence of the superior, and the terms on which his services can be secured, would even in this case be subjects on which the sociologist would be bound to bestow the same attention as he bestows at present on the activities of the ordinary men; and unless he should do this, his conclusions would be wholly valueless.

As a matter of fact, however, the hypothesis that the superior few are ever the mere passive agents which the democratic theory assumes them to be is false; and it is as a rule false in exact proportion to the difficulty and importance of the cases to which it is applied. The qualities which enable men to organise the opinions of others are usually qualities which endow them with strong opinions of their own; and in addition to their own opinions, these men, with their exceptional vigour, have usually their own purposes also; and the popular will, as put into execution by them, is always modified, and very often metamorphosed, by what they themselves add to or subtract from it. Still it must be admitted that, in spite of their dependence on the few, the many can, and do to a great extent, impress their own genuine will—the will and wishes of the average man as distinct from the will and wishes of the man who is in any way exceptional—on the exceptional men to whom their power is surrendered. The acts of the governing few may never entirely represent  the will and wishes of the average man, when these acts are considered as a whole; but they may be forced to embody, and they generally do embody, a certain element of what average men wish and will; and their character as a whole is profoundly modified in consequence. The question then is simply a question of degree. What is the extent—or rather what is the utmost possible extent—of this genuine power of the many to make the faculties of the exceptional few their servants? Is it great or small?

The reader will perceive that when this question is asked our inquiry is gradually taking a new turn, and that having started with asserting the claims of the great man as the author and sustainer of both intellectual and economic progress, we are led, when we come to consider him as an agent in the domain of politics, to inquire into what is done by the average man, as well as into what is done by him. And the reason for this is that in the domain of politics the many, so far as direct and intentional influence is concerned, are actually capable of playing a far larger part than they are in the domain of speculation or of advanced economic production. A statesman like Mr. Gladstone might, without absurdity, maintain that he had a mandate from the many to grant home-rule to Ireland; but nobody could pretend that any body of mechanics had given Watt a mandate to invent the steam-engine, or that any one gave Newton a mandate to discover the law of gravitation. And yet the reflection will probably force itself upon every reader that if the many play a part in politics which is commensurate with that of the few, they play a part in intellectual and economic progress also. It would be useless for the few to unfold their thoughts and their discoveries to the many, if the many were not, in various degrees, capable of assimilating and responding to them. Still less could the great man of industry realise his progressive inventions, or carry out his extending schemes of business, if it were not that an indefinite number of ordinary men—those "serviceable animals," as Mr. John Morley calls them—were endowed with capacities that enabled them to carry out his bidding. What would Mahomet have done if he had not had followers? What would Columbus have done if he had not had seamen? The reader, accordingly, will inevitably be led to urge that in attributing to the great men of the world the results which we have attributed to them, our statements are unmeaning, unless they are accepted as incomplete, and are understood to imply more than they have actually expressed. If no progress of any kind could have taken place without the many, surely, it will be argued, the many must have had some share in producing it; and unless we can assert and discriminate precisely what this share is—what are the phenomena of progress which are due to the activity of ordinary men—it is meaningless to assert that most of them are due to the activity of exceptional men.

And the larger part of this argument is perfectly true. In dealing with the activities of the few, we have taken those of the many for granted. This general assumption, however, though inevitable at the beginning of our inquiry, has been provisional only. To any scientific conception of what is done exclusively by the few, an equally scientific conception of what is done by the many is essential. We must measure the former by the latter, as we measure mountains by their respective heights above the sea-level. That such a discrimination between the work of these two bodies is possible may be doubted by some; and accordingly before we actually proceed to undertake it, we will dispose of the arguments that will be, and actually have been, advanced in proof of its impracticability, and set forth the principles on which it must be, and obviously can be, made.

www.ingramcontent.com/pod-product-compliance
Lightning Source LLC
LaVergne TN
LVHW041323140925
821045LV00015B/1300